HEALING FOR R.A.S.H.E.K.A.

HEALING FOR R.A.S.H.E.K.A.

MOVING FROM A
RUN AWAY SOUL HURT
EVERY KIND AWAY TO A
REFRESHED ANOINTED SOUL
HEALED EVERY KIND AWAY

JOSEPH K. WILLIAMS SR., MDIV

HEALING FOR R.A.S.H.E.K.A.
Copyright © 2021 Joseph K. Williams Sr.
All rights reserved.

Published by Publish Your Gift®
An imprint of Purposely Created Publishing Group, LLC

No part of this book may be reproduced, distributed or transmitted in any form by any means, graphic, electronic, or mechanical, including photocopy, recording, taping, or by any information storage or retrieval system, without permission in writing from the publisher, except in the case of reprints in the context of reviews, quotes, or references.

Printed in the United States of America

ISBN: 978-1-64484-339-0 (print)
ISBN: 978-1-64484-340-6 (ebook)

Special discounts are available on bulk quantity purchases by book clubs, associations and special interest groups. For details email: sales@publishyourgift.com or call (888) 949-6228.

For information log on to www.PublishYourGift.com

I dedicate this book to my mother, Carol Delores Garlic Williams. At the time of this writing, she is in the latter stages of dementia with senility. I pray daily that she will have a quality of life that gives her the "happy, happy, joy, joy" that she refers to during our conversations. She has raised me to never give up and to never give in. I watch her fight a disease that she cannot defeat. She inspires me because she continues to fight. Ma, you may not know who I am, but the world will know that you raised me to be a man who impacts people across communities, countries, and continents. The legacy I will leave is because of the lasting values that you as a strong Black woman have instilled in me. Dementia has not been able to diminish the mannerisms and looks that you have become known for over the course of your life. You are and will always be my inspiration. I love you MamaSon!

Your son,
Kevin

Table of Contents

Introduction 1

Part I: Overcoming the Hurt 7
    Chapter 1: God Is Paying Attention 9
    Chapter 2: God Is Calling You to Arise 21
    Chapter 3: God Made You an Accomplished
    Individual 35

Part II: Hunting for Healing 45
    Chapter 4: It's Time for You to Advance 47
    Chapter 5: It's Not Too Late 59

Part III: The Pathway to Healing 71
    Chapter 6: Dealing with the Necessary 73
    Chapter 7: Helpful Thoughts for Continued Healing 83

Sources 89

About the Author 91

Introduction

I received a telephone call recently from my oldest daughter. She shared with me that my first cousin's son was killed at a shopping center known as Eastover. My feelings were a mixture of pain and anger. I felt pain for my aunt because of the pain she was experiencing in the loss of a grandchild. I felt anger because of the lack of energy, that we as a family, had put toward helping my cousin's son avoid such an ending. I wondered what the driving force behind his pain was. I reached out to my cousin's sister. I told her that I was struggling with her nephew's death because we did nothing to stop it when we saw the writing on the wall thirteen years ago. Her response was telling: "The thing with him is that he was born with some mental illness that both his parents refused to deal with and accept as his reality." When people refuse to deal with and accept their pain, they mask it in many ways. It is masked in relationships, it is masked under the cover of vices, and it is masked through the transferal of pain.

The state of America in 2021 is that we are amid a tri-pandemic era. There is the health pandemic of COVID-19, or the coronavirus. At the time of this writing, it has infected half a million children in the United States. It has killed more than six hundred thousand individuals in the United States, and more than four million people have died worldwide. We are also in a pandemic of racial injustice against people of color in America.

Additionally, we are in a socioeconomic pandemic. The virus and racial disparities have impacted people of color financially and socially with more of a burden than white America.

Over the last six years, the following people of color, amongst many others, have been killed by police officers: George Floyd, Breonna Taylor, Atatiana Jefferson, Aura Rosser, Stephen Clark, Botham Jean, Philando Castile, Alton Sterling, Michelle Cusseaux, Freddy Gray, Tanisha Fonville, Eric Garner, Akai Gurley, Gabriella Nevarez, Tamir Rice, Michael Brown, and Tanisha Anderson. Their names have become pain points for people of color, and for African Americans specifically.

People are living in a climate of pain that we must get a handle on before it overthrows our moral fabric and deepens the social divide that exists in America. When I hear people say "when we get to the other side of this pandemic," I caution them and encourage them to develop a different mindset. It is important to understand that God never calls us to *get* through what we are going through. In fact, God calls us to *grow* through what we are going through. If you are spending your energy to "get through," then you are not focused on becoming a different person based on your present experience. I submit that if Americans do not grow as a result of the climate of the country, we will continue to show the same behaviors that landed us in this tri- pandemic state of being. As my grandmother always said, "when you know better, you do better."

Pain is a part of life. As it says in the song "Joy and Pain" by the R&B group Maze, featuring Frankie Beverly, "Joy and pain are like sunshine and rain." What you do with the pain or allow it to do to you is important. *Healing for R.A.S.H.E.K.A.* is about helping you overcome your pain and begin a healing process that brings you peace. All of us have been in circumstances where pain has come crashing down in our lives. Many of us have derailing moments as a result of pain, because we do not understand how to move beyond the problems that led to the painful position. According to Dr. David D. Burns in his book *Feeling Good: The New Mood Therapy*, "The first principle of cognitive therapy is that *all* your moods are created by your 'cognitions,' or thoughts. A cognition refers to the way you look at things—your perceptions, mental attitudes, and beliefs. It includes the ways you interpret things—what you say about something or someone to yourself."

Many of us have missing links in our lives. Boys grow up to be men who have trouble relating to other men because they lack a strong male role model during their upbringing. Girls begin to look for love in all the wrong places because they lacked attention in their influential years, and it now manifests as a core behavior as they walk into adulthood. Families perpetuate generational pain because they refuse to deal with the abuse that divided them decades ago and thus create dysfunctional relationships.

The African American culture, which has always been under siege, needs healing on so many fronts. We have economic pain, social justice pain, political pain, historical pain, and personal pain. In this book, we will review a passage from the Hebrew text of Genesis and look at the plight of Hagar and her son Ishmael; we will walk through the biblical text and outline key suggestions that can be used to confront those pain points that keep you from maximizing your potential. I define the key suggestions as "the healing process." We will then back up to an earlier part in the book of Genesis, supply a succession plan to help you maintain your momentum, and end with Jesus' triumph through the pain of betrayal to help you maintain your traction on the pathway of the healing process.

Pain goes beyond class and culture. It goes beyond race and creed. It is universal between the *haves* and *have nots*. Pain cannot be addressed in isolation, and it takes more than human effort to eradicate it and curtail its impact in our lives. In his book *Strength to Love*, Dr. Martin Luther King Jr. says, "The God whom we worship is not a weak and incompetent God. He is able to beat back gigantic waves of opposition and to bring low prodigious mountains of evil. The ringing testimony of the Christian faith is that God is able."

Alia Chughtai and Ai Jazeera created an online document entitled *Know Their Names*. They chronicle with words and pictures the individuals who were killed by police since 2015. They remind us that seventeen Black men and Black women have had their lives shortened because police used excessive force during their encounter. This is nothing new for the African American community, and with it comes a generational pain that rips at the fabric of our very being. When I think of these seventeen individuals, I am reminded of a different pain: the self-inflicted pain that comes from the senseless violent acts that African Americans experience in our communities. There is the violence caused by the imbalance of the educational system that our children experience early in their youth. This violence leads to an unprepared state for college and the workforce and places us behind the curve. There is the violence of socioeconomic suppression. This violence leads us into a social status of the poor, the lower class, and a separate class that positions us to be the borrower and not the lender. This violence leads to a pain that becomes constant. This violence leads to a pain that becomes the norm, and not the exception. The year 2020 can be labeled as the year of pain, and the year 2021 is a continuation. As much as people wanted to move beyond the health pandemic, it continues with a new variant that vaccines may not be able to handle. We face a health pandemic that has caused pain physically, emotionally, and socially. We also face the pandemic of racial disparity that has reminded African Americans that we are *not* living in a post-racial society. Furthermore, the election of Donald Trump as president was a "whitelash" response to the presidency of Barack Obama and caused a societal regression that reminds us of the pictures from the 1960s when white folk let the dogs loose, with fire hoses and scare tactics.

When I worked for Covenant House Washington, I served in the position of Pastoral Minister and as the Director of Street and Community Outreach over a ten-year period. I was commonly referred to as "Pastor Joe." I spent many hours providing guidance and reassurance to runaway, homeless, and at-risk youth who lived east of the Anacostia River in the District of Columbia. I spent countless hours helping them to control their anger by navigating their pain. I recall an incident with a young lady outside the DC Superior Court building. She was clearly upset because of the court proceeding she had to attend. She had her son with her, who was hungry and kept tugging on her. To quiet him, she gave him a mini box of cereal. The three-year-old found a space, took his box of cereal, and poured it out on the ground, and then went ahead to eat the cereal. When I brought it to her attention, she looked at me and said, "God made dirt and dirt don't hurt." Her pain was placed on her son because of the pain she endured from her son's father. Pain left unchecked will be misplaced throughout your life.

The title of this book can cause one to think that it is directed at women (after all, Rasheka is a female name), but it is not. R.A.S.H.E.K.A. is used as an acronym, which means Run Away Soul Hurt Every Kind Away. It is gender neutral. Everyone experiences pain that is buried deeply within us. At some point in our lives, we have been R.A.S.H.E.K.A. If you have rebelled and are now living a life of regret, you are R.A.S.H.E.K.A. If you have been in a cycle of unsuccessful relationships and cannot seem to get off the merry-go-round, you are R.A.S.H.E.K.A. If present actions remind you of past hurts, you are R.A.S.H.E.K.A. From the outset, I want you to know that your name can remain the same, but the meaning that you give your name does not have to remain the same. That thought is embedded in the title of the book.

God wants to unlock the cell door and release you from the pain that is keeping you in prison. Exodus 3:7 (NKJV) states, "And the Lord said: 'I have surely seen the oppression of My people who are in Egypt, and have heard their cry because of their taskmasters, for I know their sorrows.'" I believe that God and I together are a majority. I believe that for you also. Let the healing begin!

PART I
Overcoming the Hurt

Chapter 1

God Is Paying Attention

"And God heard the voice of the lad. Then the angel of God called to Hagar out of heaven, and said to her, "What ails you, Hagar? Fear not, for God has heard the voice of the lad where he is."

—Genesis 21:17 (NKJV)

Let me tell you about the biblical story of Abraham, Sarah, and Hagar. If there ever was a soap opera and dramatic series, their story fits the bill. God comes into the lives of an older, childless couple, Abraham and Sarah, with words of strong determination: "I will make you a great nation; I will bless you and make your name great; and you shall be a blessing" (Genesis 12:2, NKJV). So, this old couple trusts God and leans into the covenant that God makes with Abraham. They go for the whole lot: name change, location change, and the fact that God was going to make them a great nation. Mind you, they had no children, and both were past the baby-making, baby-birthing stage. Still, Abraham believed God and followed Him faithfully. He was faithful, but not faultless.

On the promises front, Sarah grows impatient with God delivering on the promise of her getting pregnant and bearing Abraham a child. So, over breakfast she says to him, "See now, the Lord has restrained me from bearing children. Please, go in to my maid; perhaps I shall obtain children by her" (Genesis 16:2b, NKJV). Of course, Abraham listened to Sarah and married Hagar, and she bore him a son named Ishmael. Sarah's pain of not being able to bear a child turns into anger toward Abraham, however, and she proceeded to basically say to Abraham—you are supposed to be a man of faith! Why could you not wait on God? In Genesis 16:5 (NKJV), Sarah yells at Abraham: "Then Sarai said to Abram, 'My wrong be upon you! I gave my maid into your embrace; and when she saw that she had conceived, I became despised in her eyes. The Lord judge between you and me.'" The circumstances become more difficult when Sarah gives birth to Isaac and subsequently tells Abraham that Hagar and her son must leave the house. The story picks up in Genesis 21. Sarah tells Abraham, "'Cast out this bondwoman and her son; for the son of this bondwoman shall not be heir with my son, namely with Isaac'" (Genesis 21:10, NKJV). This is when anger and pain overlap. Sarah is feeling the pain of regret. Abraham is feeling the pain of remorse. Hagar is feeling the pain of rejection. There is a truth in this story that many of us do not like to discuss. Their emotional, sociological, and physical pain present a platform for our discussion.

When we are experiencing emotional pain, it affects all of our relationships. It affects the relationship we have with ourselves and with others. Rejection can create internal feelings that determine how much we "give" in relationships. If we are afraid of being rejected by people, we will also protect ourselves by limiting the extent of the relationship. I call this "relationship rationing." In *Strength to Love*, Dr. Martin Luther King Jr. states, "The church today is challenged to proclaim God's Son, Jesus Christ, to be the hope of men in all of their complex personal and social problems. . . . Many young people who knock on the door are perplexed by the uncertainties of life, confused by daily disappointments, and disillusioned by the ambiguities of history." When we are afraid of being rejected by people, we put up walls of protection that do not allow people to develop an intimate connection with us. But there is a pathway to healing.

I want you to know that God is paying attention to your pain. In the Genesis story, the first thing we are told after Hagar experienced rejection is that "God heard the voice of the lad." We can overcome our pain when we realize that God is always listening. And He is not only listening; He is listening from His position of strength. When God listens to our circumstances, He is paying close attention to the internal and external sounds that we make. He attentively gives ear to our causes and pain by becoming a pilaster or fanatical supporter. You can think of God as an oak tree or a sturdy tree whose roots run deep. He is listening to your loud outburst and your silent tears. It does not matter whether you are old or young; your sounds ring out to God, and His ear is up close and personal to your pain. Psalm 139:7–8 (NKJV) states, "Where can I go from Your Spirit? Or where can I flee from your presence? If I ascend into heaven, You are there; if I make my bed in hell, behold, You are there." In order to get to a place where the healing process can begin, we must recognize that God is always listening and that we are never out of reach of His listening ear.

I have said this before and it is worth repeating: if we do not transform our pain, we will always transmit it. There are people who live in their pain and do not allow God's willingness to pay attention to be a healing balm. The biblical image of the priest laying hands on the scapegoat at the edge of the city gates, placing the sins of the people on the goat, comes to mind when I think of people walking in their pain. Using a scapegoat is our preferred method. When we deny our pain and suffering, we use the scapegoat as the rationale to project them elsewhere. America was experiencing this very thing from the person who was sitting in the highest office in the land. In an interview with CNN when talking about his book *Rage*, Bob Woodward said, "I don't know, to be honest, whether he's got it straight in his head what is real and what is unreal." America confronted this pain through our right to vote and continues to pay attention to the "new" voting regulations that attempt to limit people's impact at the ballot box. I passionately believe that to be healed, you must confront the source of your pain. That is why it is important to exercise the right to vote. It gives you the opportunity to confront the source of your political and social pain points.

The next comforting factor of God paying attention to your pain is to know that He is not only listening, but He is also looking into your circumstance. Furthermore, God is not only looking, He is also looking like a strong supporter. Often we believe that no one understands or "feels" our pain. When the "angel of God called to Hagar," it was an indication of an ensuing encounter. It was not accidental or by chance. It was an "instant message" that bypassed the email and cell phone. It was an indication of motioning toward her. In fact, it was in response to Hagar's quiescent position. The word *quiescent* means to be marked by inactivity. Hagar had become homeless and isolated. The pain caused by the eviction created a dynamic that she had not faced before. She had become paralyzed because what she had thought to be love, comfort, and family had been stripped away. When we are isolated, we're at more risk of listening to lies about who we are and coming to believe the lies as the truth.

Here is an underlying truth to Hagar's pain: She was Abraham's second wife. She was a servant. It was not God's intention that she bear a child by Abraham (that was Sarah's and Abraham's idea). She gave birth as a slave, which meant that her son was a slave as well. Hagar was cast out completely and permanently and made to be a single parent because of a circumstance in her life that she had no control over. Those are real pain points. There are many today who have a terribly similar experience as Hagar: The pain of abuse. The pain of abandonment. The pain of an absent father. These can make you believe that you are walking alone in life. One of the things that you cannot allow is for these things (and they are real things) to put you in what I define as the "burden box." In his book *Strength to Love*, Dr. King talks about different responses to pain: "One possible reaction is to distill all our frustrations into a core of bitterness and resentment. The person who pursues this path is likely to develop a callous attitude, a cold heart, and a bitter hatred toward God, toward those with whom he loves, and toward himself." To know that you are not alone in your pain, to understand that God has placed caring people in your life despite the rejection that has occurred, can serve as a springboard to your healing. Most of us spend so much time hating things about ourselves that we do not realize that we are crippling our ability to love ourselves and to love others. When you realize that God is paying attention through the lens of His eyes, it will change your perspective and help you to find rest.

Over the years, I have attended many conferences and seminars. I remember attending a seminar that was led by Pastor Charles (Chuck) Swindoll during the Pastor's Leadership Conference in 2002, and I wrote down this statement he made: "God never asked us to meet life's pressures and demands on our own terms or by relying upon our own strength. Nor did He demand that we win His favor by assembling an impressive portfolio of good deeds. Instead, He invites us to enter His rest." God is looking at your circumstances daily and is a strong supporter so that you can find relief and rest. Matthew 11:28 (NKJV) says, "Come to Me, all you who labor and are heavy laden, and I will give you rest."

When God pays attention to your pain, He does so with an empathetic longing that demonstrates His embracing of your pain from your position. We all have said to someone, "I feel you." But when God says "I feel you," He speaks it from your created position. He avouches on your behalf. The word *avouch* means to declare as a matter of fact or as a thing that can be proved. The question the angel asked Hagar was a fair question:

"What ails you, Hagar?" It not only was a fair question, it was the question that mattered to her the most. It was God's way of demonstrating that His intent toward Hagar was to show that her pain mattered. When you are at your lowest, you need to hear that you matter. Tamala Mann sings a song entitled "Take Me to the King." There is a verse in the song that says, "Truth is I'm tired. Options are few. I'm trying to pray, but where are you? I'm all churched out. Hurt and abused. I can't fake, what's left to do?" I have been there many times in my life. During those moments, I have found God's longing toward me and the things that concern me to be comforting. In her book *Acts of Faith: Daily Meditations for People of Color*, Iyanla Vanzant states in her introduction that it's necessary to "rechannel your thinking. Stress will not go away until you decide it no longer has a place in your life. Obstacles and challenges will not stop until your perception of them changes." The source of your pain does not have to maintain control over you and your life.

The final aspect of God paying attention to your situation is noted in the statement "fear not, for God has heard the voice of the lad where he is." When God pays attention to your pain, He knows your location. Because God is omnipresent, He can hear your cry and Ishmael's cry at the same time. The comfort that Hagar found lies in the fact that God kept one eye on her and the other eye on the thing that she loved the most: her son. Here she was, at her wits' end, and the God of the universe was giving her attention. Here is an interesting thought: Hagar was so focused on the cry of Ishmael that she could not recognize that God was paying attention. She saw God through the lens of Abraham and

Sarah. At this stage of the game, she wanted nothing to do with their God. God knew that she had been hurt by people of faith. He knew that "church folk" were mean and lacking compassion. By letting her know that He "heard the voice of the lad," He was lowering the noise that was clanging loud in her heart and head.

There are many single women who are playing the dual role of mother and father. My New Testament seminary professor at Howard University, the late Dr. Cain Hope Felder, states in his book *Troubling Biblical Waters: Race, Class, and Family*, "The family begins with the woman when she gives birth to the child. This is no less true of the Church as family, for, while Joseph's caring and protective role is important, everything begins with Mary, who gives birth to the Christ Child." The African American woman has had to bear the brunt of responsibility for raising our children in our communities. The pain that they have experienced because of broken relationships has impacted our family structures, and splintered the psyche of our children. Yet God is pointing out through the life of Hagar that He was paying attention back then and He is paying attention right now. He is listening. He is looking. He is longing to let you know that He "feels you." More importantly, He knows your location and the location of the things that are most important to you. In the hymn "Just a Little Talk with Jesus," there is a line in the chorus that says, "He will hear our faintest cry, He will answer by and by." Job 34:27–28 (TLB) says, "For they turned aside from following him, causing the cry of the poor to come to the attention of God. Yes, He hears the cries of those being oppressed." For me, faith and hope are rooted in the conviction that, regardless of how bad things may be, a new story is waiting to take hold and come into play. It will be something we have yet to see, feel, or experience. As Isaiah 43:19 (NKJV) declares, "Behold, I will do a new thing, Now it shall spring forth; Shall you not know it? I will even make a road in the wilderness *And* rivers in the desert." God is paying attention!

The Recapture

God is paying attention:
He is listening to you
He is looking at you
He is longing for you
He knows your location

Chapter 2

God Is Calling You to Arise

"Arise, lift up the lad and hold him with your hand, for I will make him a great nation."

—Genesis 21:18 (NKJV)

Pain can be an immobilizing emotion. It can cause people to develop insecurities that—without understanding the root cause—will make no sense to the person or persons who are impacted by the resulted behavior. I remember a relationship in which I was subjected to someone's pain and I could not understand why there was so much insecurity. We could be enjoying a wonderful atmosphere filled with laughter and fun, but then, on the way home, she would complain that I was engaging in conversation too long with people, or that she did not like how a particular person was looking at me. After we decided to go our separate ways, I learned that she was living in the pain of past relationships. It did not matter how much respect I demonstrated or how well I treated her, I could not break down that wall from the outside. That wall had to be broken down from the inside.

God has given us the free will to choose the doors we go through without having to worry that we will find ourselves outside of His will on the other side. One of the things I have learned in life is that just because I have a particular feeling, that does not mean that I must give in to it and live by that feeling. Whether you realize it or not, you are on a journey, and God is on that journey with you. To move beyond your pain, you must realize two things: 1) waiting is a part of the process, and 2) God is calling you to arise from the ashes of your pain. Betty Skinner, the subject of the book *The Hidden Life: Awakened* by Kitty Crenshaw and Cathy Snapp, articulated it this way: "Waiting is one of the most difficult pieces of a deep, inner spiritual journey. We want to outrun God, but our growth depends on consciously letting go of our fear and allowing our circumstances the space to teach us what God intends.... As long as we are still waiting in fear and anxiety, we will not experience growth."

There are four dynamics that are involved in your ability to arise from the ashes of your pain. For you to understand the forthcoming dynamics, you must realize that these dynamics are not optional if you want to walk in your healing. In fact, it is imperative to understand that Genesis 21:18 begins with a command. When we think of a command, we automatically think of someone having dominance and influence over us. With God, there is another aspect that we should consider. The word also means to influence from a strategic position. That recalls God's relationship with Joshua. In my mind, the epitome of that relationship is embodied in Joshua 1:9 (NKJV): "Have I not commanded you? Be strong and of good courage; do not be afraid, nor be dismayed, for the Lord your God is with you wherever you go." Notice the intonation of the verse? God is commanding but guiding. God is commanding but reassuring. God is commanding but loving.

The first dynamic is that God is calling you to get up. Now, I do not want to state this in a manner that might make it seem matter-of-fact. All of us have had that dream where we felt like someone or something was holding us down and not allowing us to move. Yes, moving beyond your pain is a journey. The key to understanding what it means to get up lies in the fact that you do have the ability to get up. Hagar is challenged by the angel to get up. This is a literal, figurative, intensive, and causative command that is calling for an action by her. The expectation is for her to move in a manner as if she were roused. The word *rouse* is the root of arouse, meaning to be awakened with excitement. The archaic meaning is defined as to cause to break from cover. In other words, the dynamic of getting up is calling you to break from the cover of your pain. Your pain has been a mask that does not reveal your true identity. Many times, we need help or a friend for support. In his book *Chazown: Discover and Pursue God's Purpose for Your Life*, Craig Groeschel recounts the interaction of David and Jonathan from 1 Samuel 23:16. He states, "One man helped another man find strength—not in self-determination, not in an army, not in positive thinking—but in God." If you allow people to get close enough to you, you will find that God has aligned someone who genuinely cares about you.

The second dynamic that will help you to arise is the need for you to go on. In the previous verse, Hagar had placed Ishmael under a bush and sat a "stone's throw" away from him. God changed that dynamic by reminding her that she had to advance and not stand still. Her instruction is to "lift up the lad." When you stand still after being hurt, all you can feel is the pain that the hurt has delivered to your psyche and heart. Being paralyzed by pain is real. How many relationships have you shut the door on because of your pain? How many of your friends have you watched destroy relationships because they lack the ability to recognize that years of past pain are the governing motor of their present days? Here is the key to "go on": you must *lose yourself*. What does that mean? In the text, the first command of the angel was directed to Hagar, but the subsequent words were directed at Ishmael. To *lose oneself* is to understand that while your life matters—and it does—your life is also meant to matter to others. Your life cannot matter to others if you are paralyzed by pain. The decision you must make is which role you want to play in life. Do you want to play the role of the victim or the victor? In this time of racial equity and inclusion efforts and the racial divide that was created from the presidency of Donald Trump, I am amazed how white people want to flip the script and now become the victim. In the 1960s and 1970s, racism was hidden. But, as Robin DiAngelo says in her book *White Fragility: Why It's So Hard for White People to Talk About Racism*, "Today we have a cultural norm that insists we hide our racism from people of color and deny it among ourselves, but not that we actually challenge it." You need to flip the script internally; do not hide your pain, do not deny your pain, but challenge your pain while putting your focus on something outside of yourself. I am reminded of a time in King David's life (before he became King) when the pain was so great that he was literally ready to give up completely.

The Bible speaks of him being greatly distressed. You can say it with me: been there, done that! The key was his action following that moment. In 1 Samuel 30:6 (NKJV), it states, "Now David was greatly distressed, for the people spoke of stoning him, because the soul of all the people was grieved, every man for his sons and his daughters. But David strengthened himself in the Lord his God." God is ready to make you happy and whole. God is ready to take your pain away and replace it with joy. That is how you go on.

The next dynamic involves a tool I call "gather in." In the *arise* process, getting up and going on are critical, but understanding the need to gather in is crucial. Why? Because it involves you transforming your mental approach toward your pain. When you have allowed your pain to lead you daily, it strangles your psyche. Hagar is instructed to "hold him with your hand." I have a picture outside of my home office door of an African American man holding an infant close to him. Whether you are male or female, there is an internal transformation that takes place when you hold a child in your arms. You feel the sense of responsibility and the need to care for another human being. Mentally, you realize that this child needs the best you have to offer so that he/she may grow into a self-sufficient adult. Hagar's directive from the angel requires Hagar to fasten her eyes upon Ishmael with a courageous spirit. The directive involves several factors, and when you follow them, they bring about a mental change in your thought process and how you deal with your pain.

I became a father at the age of sixteen. When I went to Washington Hospital Center to pick up my daughter, she was three days old. I realized that while I was a growing boy on the outside, I needed to mentally be a responsible man. The days of pursuing football and baseball ended with the bundle of joy that was in my young hands. I had summoned myself to the role to "be the man." I could have looked at myself as a statistic; that was the expected norm of growing up in southeast District of Columbia. There were supporting external factors that would have supported my mentality. At that time, for all that I attended Catholic school, my relationship with God was very much a surface relationship. My dependence upon His power was nil to none. I could have given in to the prevailing pain that was engulfing my community. Fortunately, I had a mother who was a strong Black woman that was fortified with enough God and will to direct me otherwise. One of the tools that will help you to gather in is to understand the word obstinate. In the pure since of the word, we know *obstinate* to mean stubbornly adhering to an opinion, purpose, or course despite reason, arguments, or persuasion. A second definition brings this word into our context: not easily subdued, remedied, or removed. The hymn "I Shall Not Be Moved" declares it best in the chorus of the song: "Just like a tree planted by the rivers of waters, I shall not be moved." To obtain this internal posture, you need to develop fortitude or the will to push your psyche past your pain. In her book *Acts of Faith*, Iyanla Vanzant states, "Growing brighter and more brilliant each day, you can accept the truth of who you are. The next time you want to know who you are, what you are or if something is the right thing to do, don't ask your neighbor—ask the power within . . . and pay attention to the response!" The art of gathering in will help you to garner the strength to arise from your pain and behave valiantly.

The next directive that will help you to arise from your pain lies in your ability to grasp purpose and understand providence. Many people who are immersed in pain cannot see purpose and providence. Purpose involves goal setting with a focus to achieve something. Providence is the fact that God is conceived as the power sustaining and guiding human destiny. These two intersect when Hagar is told "for I will make him a great nation." When we discussed the interactions between Abraham, Sarah, and Hagar, we called to attention that Abraham was the father of faith. Through him was to be the promised seed (Isaac) that was to give life to the covenant that God had with Abraham. While Ishmael was not a part of God's directive (the promise child), he was still a part of God's providence. I believe that there are things that happen in life that are in either God's perfect will or God's permissive will. God promised Abraham a thing. Abraham and Sarah decided that they could not wait on God's perfect will. Abraham and Sarah decided to help God out and brought Hagar into the picture, and thus created the scenario of God's permissive will. The source of Hagar's pain was the choice made by Abraham and Sarah. Yet God looked beyond the problem they created and the pain they caused and set a course for, gave a purpose to, Ishmael. No matter who you are or what situation you were "birthed" in, God will provide a pathway that will help you to overcome your pain and propel you to a place of healing. Jeremiah 29:11 (NKJV) serves as a constant reminder to me that God is always working to make things better in life. It states, "For I know the thoughts that I think toward you, says the Lord, thoughts of peace and not of evil, to give you a future and a hope." Grasp purpose and providence and you will arise to a position that is above your pain.

The final directive that will give you the ability to rise is something that many of us do not want to do. That is to grow up. It takes a mature individual to transition their mindset from being a victim to becoming the victor. For that matter, the same applies to communities and cultures. Amid the COVID-19 virus crises, there are clinical vaccine trials that are taking place. African Americans are reluctant to participate in the clinical trials because we still remember the Tuskegee experiment. The following is a recap of that experience from history, taken from the CDC's "The Tuskegee Timeline":

> In 1932, the Public Health Service, working with the Tuskegee Institute, began a study to record the natural history of syphilis in hopes of justifying treatment programs for blacks. It was called the "Tuskegee Study of Untreated Syphilis in the Negro Male." The study initially involved 600 black men—399 with syphilis, 201 who did not have the disease. The study was conducted without the benefit of patients' informed consent. Researchers told the men they were being treated for "bad blood," a local term used to describe several ailments, including syphilis, anemia, and fatigue. In truth, they did not receive the proper treatment needed to cure their illness. In exchange for taking part in the study, the men received free medical exams, free meals, and

burial insurance. Although originally projected to last six months, the study actually went on for forty years.

As a collective people, we have developed a mistrust of government-sponsored trials because of that experience. In a conversation with African American clergy leaders, the question was asked as to what could be done to get more African Americans to participate in the clinical trials. The responses varied from building confidence to creating knowledge to building trust. My response was to challenge our community to grow up. Now, my response seemed to discount the facts that African American are greatly and disproportionately impacted by the COVID-19 virus and were deceived greatly during the Tuskegee experiment. In my mind, though, it is not a disregard, but an acknowledgment of the facts that are before us. We have the need to know that the vaccine will work for African Americans, as with all Americans.

When you are immersed in your pain, it is natural to develop a mistrust for everyone around you. In fact, even people who are not the author of your pain become equated with the original perpetrators by virtue of association. If they behave similarly to or say some of the same things as the person or thing that caused your pain, they take you back to the original place of your pain. Hagar had to face her pain and was forced to grow up so that Ishmael could be positioned to live in purpose and providence. She had to grow up from being the discounted slave girl to being the mother of a man who would be a "great nation." Hagar's view of herself was both internal and external. Internally she adopted the identity of being a slave girl, and externally she received ill treatment from Sarah (which was allowed by Abraham). A part of her growing up was moving from hate to love. Hagar had to stop hating herself and forgive Sarah for the mistreatment that was created by a jealous spirit. While this is challenging, it is necessary to mature as an individual. Dr. King once said, "Along the way of life, someone must have sense enough and morality enough to cut off the chain of hate. This can be done only by projecting the ethics of love to the center of our lives." I have learned in my own journey that authentic spirituality is always first about you—about allowing your own heart and mind to be changed. The decision to mature or grow up beyond your pain is significant because it is a sign that you desire to maximize your potential. To maximize your potential, there must be a strong element of the love of self. Many marriages are struggling, and the divorce rate has skyrocketed when compared to March 2019 through June 2019. When there is a lack of self-love, love is not the prevailing effort in relationships. In his book *Secrets to Lasting Love: Uncovering the Keys to Lifelong Intimacy*, Gary Smalley hits the nail on the head when he states that "if you're not continually nurturing and deepening your relationship, you may be lighting the fuse on a time bomb that can eventually blow, breaking your home, your family, and, finally, your heart."

You were not meant to spend a lifetime in a position of pain. As a people and community, we need you to get off the sideline and get in the game. We cannot let you stay down and out! Isaiah 52:2 (NKJV) states, "Shake yourself from the dust, arise; sit down, O Jerusalem! Loose yourself from the bonds of your neck, O captive daughter of Zion!" The words of Jesus ring just as loud today as when he declared them in Mark 2:11 (NKJV): "I say to you, arise, take up your bed, and go to your house." Growing up will empower you to get up from your pain and live out the promise of God in your life.

The Recapture

God is calling you to arise:

Get up

Get on

Gather in

Grasp purpose and providence

Grow up

Chapter 3

God Made You an Accomplished Individual

"Then God opened her eyes, and she saw a well of water. And she went and filled the skin with water, and gave the lad a drink."

—Genesis 21:19 (NKJV)

When I was fourteen years old, I found out that I was adopted. I did not realize the impact that coming into that knowledge had on me until I got older. Now I want to be clear, my mother, father, aunts, uncles, and other relatives never treated me differently. In fact, I only heard the reference to me being adopted once, when my uncle was trying to help my mother (who suffers from severe dementia) to understand that I was her son. But the impact on my psyche played out in the form of feeling rejection and negatively impacted my belief in my abilities. Because I grew up east of the Anacostia River in the District of Columbia (specifically Ward 8), I was reminded of the "less than" expectation through various mediums. By the time I entered college, I was fighting internal thoughts regarding my ability to compete with fellow students. I reacted to this pain in a variety of ways. The most consistent way was by having a "chip" on my shoulder. It appeared in the form of anger and a mean personality. When I started taking relationships seriously, meaning when I started to care about women's feelings, I realized that one of my pain points was rejection by others. To this day, it is something that I must consistently work on and couch it in a way so that it does not cause internal pain. In other words, I had to come to know who I was and what my abilities are.

This is where we find Hagar in the story. It takes a lot of energy and effort to move forward, to overcome pain that has been a part of your fabric for so long a time. The best way to overcome the pain in your life, that has built a platform of lies, is by gathering facts. Your internal conversations should be based on facts, not lies or emotions. I said this before and it is worth repeating: when we are isolated, we are more at risk of listening to lies about who we are and coming to believe them as truth. Hagar had allowed the statements of being a slave, a bondwoman, a mistress, and a single parent to dance in her head too long. In the words of Melanie Fiona, Hagar was wondering "how did I become the wrong side of a love song?" But while she sat at a distance, she used that time to view her circumstances in a different light. Quiet gives you bandwidth to hear God's whispers of wisdom that are drowned out by the noise in your life. The practice of stopping and taking stock of the situation is called mindfulness. Mindfulness is mental training. The key to mindfulness is through taking control of our thoughts and through practice. Through the lens of Hagar, we see four qualities that are necessary to understand that you were created as an accomplished individual: having strength, having the ability to see clearly, understanding your source, and finding satisfaction in the process.

Hagar's mind was closed by her pain. Her pain caused her to shut down mentally, and she shut down physically with the act of sitting down to watch her son die. Pain intensifies during stressful circumstances. But when our mental faculties are shut down, God will use other means to bring us to our senses. Genesis 21:19 begins with, "Then God opened her eyes." The opening of her eyes represents a strength that she did not have previously. That strength gave her the ability to understand that she was a valued individual. When you realize that your ultimate strength is not from the relationships that rejected you, but from the God who created you in His image, you can gain strength in every circumstance. The truth of the matter is that you cannot be liberated from your circumstance by yourself. Ta-Nehisi Coates, in his book *Between the World and Me*, states, "The fact of history is that black people have not—probably no people have ever—liberated themselves strictly through their own efforts. In every great change in the lives of African Americans we see the hand of events that were beyond our individual control, events that were not unalloyed goods." Our redemptive motive has always been through the hand of God. I can recall stories from my grandparents and great-grandparents telling us how the "hand of God" got them through the end of slavery, Jim Crow, and the civil rights struggle. God has always been our strength. In fact, Psalm 18:2a (NKJV) states, "The Lord is my rock and my fortress and my deliverer; my God, my strength, in whom I will trust." You have strength to accomplish things beyond your present moment. Each day is an opportunity to showcase to yourself that you are an overcomer. I believe that until there has been a journey through pain, we do not understand the value of healing. It is during that journey that you come to know who you really are. Think about Hagar's story. She was a slave, which means she was purchased by or given to Abraham. She had to feel that the opportunity she was being afforded was a chance at a better life. Sarah's jealousy and ill treatment of her and Abraham's response of rejection wounded her severely. That pain was real. In her pain, God revealed that she had one consistent value. Her relationship with God was that constant value. When God opened her eyes, she gained strength that she did not have before. You should put this book down for a moment and thank God for your journey. When you begin to express thanks to God, your heart begins to change. The way you view life and look at situations shifts. Go ahead and thank God for the shift from pain to healing!

The second quality that led to Hagar's understanding that she was an accomplished person is that her vision allowed her to see things that her pain shielded from her. The second part of the verse says that "she saw a well of water." Previously, she was staring at death. Her pain had pinpointed her thinking on the death of her son and then her subsequent death. The ability to see differently is the key to moving beyond your pain. The important point here is the contrast between not seeing previously and seeing presently. Previously she saw death. With her eyes now open, she saw life. In this text, water represents resurgence, refreshment, and restoration. It represents life! Hagar has a shift that moves from death to life. It was God's will for Hagar and Ishmael to live, not to die! It is the same for you. The greatest decision you can make in life is to become who you already are. Hagar's ability to see represents a newfound knowledge. It should be the same for you and me. Knowledge removes the interposing object, and when we look through the bright optic glass, we can see God at work in our lives and anticipate our accomplishments with a joyous confidence. My systematic theology professor at Howard University School of Divinity, Dr. Kelly Brown-Douglas, made this statement in class several times: "Mary Magdalene and the other women were the first witness to the resurrection because they remained present for the entire process, from death unto new life. That is exactly what is necessary to witness resurrections in our own lives as well." Here are three assurances we can take confidently into our future: God is not done with us yet, He's ready to do a new thing in our lives, and He will be there every step of the way. You can see beyond your pain because God has moved you from death to life.

Now that you have strength and can see from a different perspective, it is important for you to connect to the source that brings your healing. Life has taught you that friends and family members are not your source. They can be a resource, but they are not your source. That is a fact that you must face. There is a quote from author/playwright James Baldwin that I keep up in my home office: "Not everything that is faced can be changed. But nothing can be changed until it is faced." While that statement may seem a bit harsh, it is necessary if you are going to connect with the source, God, that will bring healing. You can see a change in Hagar's disposition: "And she went and filled the skin with water." When we met her a few verses ago, she was in despair and ready to die. Now she got up despite her circumstances and had forward motion. Additionally, she did something that was not previously denoted: she used an existing resource to bring relief to her situation. Pain can cause you to think that you do not have anything to bring to the table. As a man, I believe that I have the responsibility to be the provider, protector, and prayer warrior for my family. When I am lacking in any of those areas, I begin to feel that I am not fulfilling my responsibility.

I have learned that a lack of resources does not determine my ambition. Some people cannot move forward into something new because they need to "be ready." While I agree with the need for preparation and experience, I see myself as having accomplished my ambition before it manifests itself. In my mind, I was an author before I published my first book, *Move the Needle*. It is important for me to maintain my connection to the source so that He, God, can lead me to my needed resource. God (the source) opened Hagar's eyes so that she could see a well of water (the resource). The source that provides you with the ability to achieve is your relationship with God. That is why it is vital that you move beyond your pain. If we do not transform our pain, we will transmit it in some other form or action. If you want God to address your pain, take a lesson from Hagar—listen to the voice of God.

Many of us are afraid to trust God because we are afraid that we will be disappointed and will let God down. I will let you in on a little secret that will help you to move forward: the best thing to do when fear has a stranglehold on you is to befriend someone who lives in real and constant fear. This will get you to understand the power of God's love. As you work to help someone else, God will show up in your situation and bring you hope and healing. Demonstrating love to someone else will bring a new level of understanding into your psyche. In 1 John 4:18 (NKJV), we are told, "There is no fear in love; but perfect love casts out fear, because fear involves torment. But he who fears has not been made perfect in love." Fear will keep you in darkness and perpetuate your pain.

We are experiencing an atmosphere of fear and pain in this country now. A former president was questioning the pillars of democracy, casting darkness over every aspect of systematic change, and creating a racial divide that is like-unto the 1920s. We cannot allow other people to create dark clouds in our lives to keep us from the source of life. The philosopher Carl Jung wrote in *Alchemical Studies*, volume 13 of his collected works, "One does not become enlightened by imagining figures of light, but by making the darkness conscious." Pain places you in darkness. Comprehend it. Challenge its place in your life, and you will find the light that God is pointing you toward. Revealing your feelings about yourself and your pain is the beginning of your healing. Your source is not just the voice of God, it is also the word of God as well. Psalm 119:105 (NKJV) says, "Your word is a lamp to my feet and a light to my path." The nineteenth century theologian Charles H. Spurgeon stated "whatever God has made prominent in His word, He intended to be conspicuous in our lives."

The ability to bring satisfaction to the lives of others is important. While we all know that we cannot please everyone, our actions should bring satisfaction to key individuals in our lives. I am not speaking of those difficult people in your life who need healing and do not have the ability to be satisfied. Rather, our employer, our spouse, our children, our friends, and our family members should have the expectation of a relationship that brings satisfaction. I have an accountability circle, as well as those to whom I am accountable to personally. I am accountable to my family. Additionally, I have a group of brothers who hold me accountable to my responsibilities as a man and a member of my engaged communities. My behaviors and actions are important because of our shared responsibilities. My accomplishments are necessary for the group. It is not about individual accomplishments but about those achievements that help to empower people and my community. It serves as a reminder that I am in a community, and when I begin to feel uncertain or unsure of myself, the group serves as a support. This group also challenges me when I am not living up to my potential. Instead of wearing yourself out in your struggle with your pain, understand the power of prioritizing wisdom. You will be empowered to see your way through to a successful and fulfilling life.

The Recapture

You are an accomplished individual:
God gives you strength
God grants you the ability to see
God is your source
Understand the need to be satisfying

PART II
Hunting for Healing

Chapter 4

It's Time for You to Advance

"So God was with the lad; and he grew and dwelt in the wilderness, and became an archer."

—Genesis 21:20 (NKJV)

If you have not figured it out, we are discussing aspects of the healing process. I often share with people that some things are better caught than taught. It is sometimes better for you to have your own "ah-ha" moment than to be told about one. There is truth to the statement that experience is the best teacher. When you look at your situation, it is important for you to address your disposition. Are you standing still because of your pain? Are you feeling as if you are the victim, and not victorious? I want you to know that healing begins with a step. Here is a simple thought: there is someone in your life that you know is sincere in their actions toward you. It could be a friend, spouse, or family member. They see you visibly upset and they ask if you are okay. You respond by saying "I'm fine." You both know that is not true—and that is a moment to get guidance and comfort for your pain. Your response of "I'm fine" keeps you in the same chair, looking out of the window at a depressing downpour. You cannot advance or move forward if you are not open to receiving support and help. I have heard many people say, "I am waiting on God." But Hagar would have still been sitting in her pain and Ishmael would have still been crying if she had not realized that it was time to advance.

There are three principles that I would like to share with you. These principles are simple, yet they only work if you employ them. These principles are rooted in God's love for you and will take time to become foundational in your life. Healing is a process that takes time, but it does happen with time. That is how love works. Love is painfully time-consuming. All parents know this, as do all devoted lovers and most long-term friends. There are no shortcuts. There is no life-hack, and there is no killer app. It takes an enormous amount of time to love well. Love does not come as a theory. It moves in bodies, in nature, in the ground beneath us, and in the spaces between us. Love is a different nature, waiting in us like a secret seed with the potential to give birth to our potential. The following principles will help you to move forward with confidence and assurance.

The first principle to help you to advance is to know that you have a pilaster in your life. That pilaster is God. Genesis 21:20 begins with "So God was with the lad." When we read the phrase "so God was with," it translates from the Hebrew language as "God was positioned with." The word used in the Hebrew language is "ayil" (pronounced ah-yil). It means strength, anything strong, a chief, a mighty man, a strong tree, and a pilaster. Now, I provide training across the country to houses of worship that want to understand community development. For the sake of context, community development is the building of structures that have benefit for and impact in neighborhoods. When you think of affordable housing projects, that is a form of community development. And when a structure is being built, it has a pilaster as a part of the structure. From an architectural perspective, a pilaster is treated as a column. In the structure of a building, columns serve as a strong support to the foundation of the building.

So, God was with the lad as a strong support and the foundation of his life. Ishmael was discarded by his father, but God was with him. His mother did not know how to handle their circumstance, but God was with him. He was denied his heritage, but God was with him. The ability to overcome the internal struggles in your life and gain victory over them begins with you fully devoting yourself to God and to the notion of making him Lord over your life. People will let you down, but God will be there to lift you up. Wisdom is calling you to advance. In a maternal way, she encourages us to grow up, to cast aside our immature and punitive images of God, and to be honest with ourselves about our own actions that have their roots in spiritual blindness. David declares in Psalm 27:1 (NKJV), "The Lord is my light and my salvation; whom shall I fear? The Lord is the strength of my life; of whom shall I be afraid?"

The next principle is promotion and promise. If you hear my excitement throughout this next section, then you will understand that I am passionate about this principle. Genesis 21:20 continues with "and he grew and dwelt in the wilderness." Now, before you turn your nose up at that statement, let me provide context. When you follow the story of Hagar and Ishmael, it is relational to a single mother having the responsibility of raising a son without the help of his father. Statistically, the expectation is for that child to be undereducated, underemployed, and a basic underachiever. Why? Because statistically, children who have the benefit of both parents have fared better in our society. But the wilderness represents a place full of life and opportunity. Ishmael went from death to life. He went from the pain of rejection to the place of resources. He went from having no home to having the land mass for several homes. Marvin Sapp, in his song "My Testimony," says it this way: "So glad I made it/ I made it through/ In spite of the storm and rain, heartache and pain/ I'm still alive declaring to you/ I made it through/ See, I didn't lose/ Experience lost at a major cost/ But I never lost faith in you." As long as you are still alive, you have the opportunity of promotion and promise.

You may need some assistance to get through your pain, but that should be expected. We all need support from our communities. Let me offer you this: as strong as I am individually, I realize that I am stronger collectively. Consider Ecclesiastes 4:9–10 (NKJV): "Two are better than one, because they have a good reward for their labor. For if they fall, one will lift up his companion. But woe to him who is alone when he falls, for he has no one to help him up."

I started my journey into adulthood early. I was sixteen years old and being raised by a single mother. The last thing she needed from me was to have another person to house and feed. As a teenage father who was African American, I had positioned myself to become a statistic. I needed help to find promotion and promise. When I was in my junior year at Ballou Senior

High School in Southeast, District of Columbia, my guidance counselor called me into his office and informed me that I only needed one and a half credits to finish high school. I realized in that moment the importance of connecting with people whose experiences can help to elevate you to the next level.

That was my introduction to understanding how I needed others to help me to navigate systems as an inexperienced individual. Whether you are new to the position of pain or consider yourself a veteran of hurtful circumstances, having someone to help you navigate the terrain can be helpful in positioning yourself for promotion and the fulfillment of the promise inside of you. When the prophet Elijah was weary because of his journey, he got this response from God: "And the angel of the Lord came back the second time, and touched him, and said, 'Arise and eat, because the journey is too great for you'" (1 Kings 19:7, NKJV). You need to know that God has placed people on the earth to connect with other people, to let them know that they are not alone or forgotten. They are in your life to help you find the promise that lies in you, so God can promote you to the place of healing, health, and wholeness.

The third principle is purpose and proficiency. When the healing power of God is active in your life, it serves as a vital resource to make you complete. One of the things I tell people who make the statement "I am looking for someone to complete me" is that the disposition found in that statement leads a relationship to failure. Why? Because you are already complete. My mother used to make a pound cake that she called the "five flavor pound cake." Those cakes by themselves were delicious. They were complete and did not need anything other than the original ingredients. Now, add a couple of scoops of vanilla ice cream or some sweet peaches, and it became an even better dessert! The cake flavor and the ice cream and fruit flavors came together to make the separate dishes one great dish. That brings us to the final point that will advance you in the healing process.

Genesis 21:20 closes with "and became an archer." This is a demonstration of God equipping Ishmael with purpose and proficiency—which made him complete. When we met Ishmael, his mother Hagar had placed him under a bush and he was crying. After growing in the healing process of God, though, he found God to be his strength, his pilaster, he found promotion and promise in God, and finally he found his purpose and was infused with a skillset that was twofold. Let us unpack the skillset of an archer. According to Wikipedia, "Archery, or the use of bow and arrows, was developed by the end of the Upper Paleolithic. Archery has been an important military and hunting skill for over 10,000 years and figures prominently in the mythologies of many cultures. Archers, whether on foot, in chariots or mounted on horses were a major part of most military forces. Archery is still practiced today, including in the training regime of certain special forces. It also continues to be a popular sport, most commonly in the form of target archery, but in some places also for hunting."

There are two things that come out of this summary, to be an archer is to be a warrior and to be a hunter. In his book *The Way of the Warrior: An Ancient Path to Inner Peace*, Erwin Raphael McManus states, "The warrior is not ready for battle until they have come to know peace. This is the way of the warrior." God could not entrust Ishmael with the skill set of a warrior until Ishmael made peace with the pain points in his life. He had to make peace with being born to a mother who was a slave. He had to make peace with having a father who divorced his mother because she was not primary in his life. He had to make peace with being rejected and cast out from what he knew to be home. He had to make peace with his understanding of who he was and who he was to become. That is a severe amount of pain to encounter. Yet, Ishmael "became."

What are you becoming? How are you growing? There can be no healing without internal growth. Theologian Howard Thurman, former Dean of Chapel at Howard University, said it this way: "There can be no more significant personal resolution . . . than this: I will face the problem I have been putting off because of too much fear, of too many tears, of too much resentment, even if it means crying all the way through, in order that I may [learn to] deal with it without fear, tears, or resentment." To become a warrior, you have to be sick and tired of being sick and tired! You must come to that place in your heart where you realize you were created to be more, not to be less. Ishmael found his purpose and so can you. Exodus 9:16 (NKJV) says, "But indeed for this purpose I have raised you up, that I may show My power in you, and that My name may be declared in all the earth." Your pain has to succumb to the purpose of God in you. Why? Because God wants to show you off for His glory! He wants all the earth, not just where you live, to know that you were created to make a difference *in* all the earth by the power and might of the almighty God.

When you find your purpose, you will also find the skillset, the proficiency, that will help you to achieve that purpose. Ishmael not only developed the ability to protect himself, he also had the ability to provide for himself. When Ishmael "became an archer," he went from being a whiner to being a winner. He no longer needed "mommy motivation" to handle life's circumstances. I tell my adult son that if you do not have self-motivation, you will lack the necessary spark to be a complete man. Men must move beyond their pain so that they can provide for their families, pray for their families, and protect their families. Men who are waiting on an outside influence to move them forward will remain stuck and lack purpose (read more about this in my book *Move the Needle*). God works from the inside so that we can manifest His qualities on the outside. This is called transformation. When Saul the Pharisee became the Apostle Paul, Jesus' command to him was this: "But rise and stand on your feet; for I have appeared to you for this purpose, to make you a minister and a witness both of the things which you have seen and of the things which I will yet reveal to you" (Acts 26:16, NKJV). God is ready to change your name. God is ready to reveal to you what you were born to do so that you can turn the world upside-down. There are people who are waiting on you to become healed so that they can find healing through your experience.

Your pain has given you skill sets that have yet to be evoked in your life. I remember an incident when I was nineteen and my oldest daughter was three years old. I was giving her a bath. Prior to that, I was hanging out getting high. As I was helping her to finish washing up, she looked up and said, "Daddy, what's wrong with your eyes?" It was one of those moments as a young parent in which I realized that my behavior would also chart her path in life. From that point on, I would not allow her to see any of my bad habits. It meant that I had to decrease those activities and focus on providing her with the nurturing that she needed to become well rounded. I could have told her to be quiet and ignored it, but that would have perpetuated a cycle of pain. At that time, I was an angry individual on the inside. But I did not need to channel that anger to my daughter. If my daughter was going to have a fighting chance, I needed to allow God to work in my life so that He could eventually work in her life. Now, do not get me wrong; I did not immediately stop being angry. It was (and is) a work in progress. I must intentionally work on my disposition. That is daily work, infused with daily prayer and meditation. I maintain a centered disposition so that I can support the broken people in my life who I am responsible for, and whom I am accountable to as well. The transformation of your pain to healing is not going to make you a superhero, but it will make you an ordinary hero. Those are the heroes that God uses. Jim Cymbala, in his book *Fresh Wind, Fresh Fire: What Happens When God's Spirit Invades the Hearts of His People,* states it this way: "What we desperately need in our own time are not Christians full of can't and posturing, railing at the world's problems of secular humanism, New Age, or whatever. We need men and women who will step out to turn back today's slide." I believe that Jesus usually transforms people at the moments when they most hate themselves, when they most feel shame or guilt, or want to punish themselves. When you begin to express thanks to God for healing your pain, your heart begins to change. When you do this, the way you view life and look at your situation shifts.

The Recapture

It's time for you to advance:

God is your pilaster

God has granted you promotion and promise

You are infused with purpose and proficiency

Chapter 5
It's Not Too Late

"While the earth remains, seedtime and harvest, cold and heat, winter and summer, and day and night shall not cease."

—Genesis 8:22 (NKJV)

I am going to discuss three reasons why a Run Away Soul Hurt Every Kind Away (R.A.S.H.E.K.A.) can be healed. But before I venture down that path, allow me to interject some principles about time. I have been fortunate to serve in many positions in the human service field for more than twenty-five years. I have worked with youth, young adults, adults, and older adults. While I was the Executive Director for Emmaus Services for the Aging, I was privileged to get to know many older adults who resided in the District of Columbia. Additionally, as the state president for AARP District of Columbia, I was privileged to work on behalf of older adults across eleven states in the South Region of AARP. I learned much from those individuals I served. For those older adults living their best lives, they had one common thread: they were not living to survive, but living to thrive. Just because something has had a foothold in your life over a period of time does not mean that it must remain so. Many of the older adults I encountered were progressive in their thinking and wanted to experience new challenges. Now, some were set in their ways, and that often caused them to become limited by health challenges. But others did not allow their age to determine their options in life. Time and seasons in life should not define us. After celebrating her fiftieth birthday, Jo Ann Jenkins, the CEO of AARP and author of the book *Disrupt Aging: A Bold New Path to Living Your Best Life at Every Age*, said, "I decided then and there that I wouldn't be defined by my age any more than I would be defined by my race, sex, or income. I want people to define me by *who* I am, not *how old* I am, and I refuse to allow the old expectations of what I should or should not do at a certain age define what I am going to do." There is a pathway for you to have the same disposition. I am going to outline it for you through the lens of the end of Noah's journey on the Ark.

The story of Noah is commonly known as a classic biblical story in the Old Testament or Hebrew Bible. It is filled with intrigue, deliverance, faith, and perseverance. Before God made a covenant with Abraham, He made a covenant with Noah after he, his family, and the animals came off the Ark. This covenant was with humanity and creation. This covenant has stipulations that correlate to our lives and principles that we can use on our journey to healing.

In reviewing Genesis 8:22, there are six things that God promises that are still in place today. The first promise from God is that *opportunity* will always be with us. "While the earth remains" is the foundation of that promise. Each day that we wake up is a new day of opportunity. What will you do with the opportunity that is given to you today? I do not know about you, but I choose to take full advantage of the new opportunity that I am afforded today. Recently in a conversation with a friend, I shared that in light of the number of deaths that we experienced over an eight-month timeframe during the COVID-19 virus, it is important to take each opportunity presented to me seriously. The only way you allow opportunity to bypass you is if you believe what others say versus believing what your heart says. James Baldwin, in his book *The Fire Next Time*, writes to his nephew James: "You can only be destroyed by believing that you really are what the white world calls a *nigger*. I tell you this because I love you, and please don't you ever forget it."

The second promise that God grants is that you will have *options*. "Seedtime and harvest" represents the options of fruitfulness, posterity, and the ability to reap from what has been planted. What are you planting mentally and spiritually in your life? Are you planting the seeds rooted in your pain, or are you planting the seeds rooted in your healing? The Apostle Paul encourages the church at Galatia with these words: "Do not be deceived, God is not mocked; for whatever a man sows, that he will also reap" (Galatians 6:7, NKJV). The options that God wants to make available to you are various; it is the choice and/or choices that you make that will determine if those options will help you to engage in your healing process.

The third promise that God has for you is that you will have the proper *operational temperatures*. "Cold and heat" represents a spectrum that does not involve an in-between temperature so much as it relates to your atmosphere. I live in the DMV, commonly known as the District, Maryland, and Virginia area. We are fortunate that we get changes in our environmental atmosphere. My oldest son lives in California; while he gets a calendar change, he does not get the corresponding weather. I appreciate the fact that I can experience a climate change. Why? Because at the various times of the calendar year, I know what the operational temperatures will be, and I have an appreciation for their impact upon my environment. While I am not a big fan of the cold, I realize that cold temperatures help to cleanse the air. They purify and get rid of certain bacteria that linger because of the warmer air. Because I love to play golf, I appreciate the heat that comes with the spring and summer seasons. It means that I can play golf as much as my schedule allows. Proper *operational temperatures* are God's way of providing you with temperature changes in your life that provide the proper remedy at the proper time. Most people will not wear shorts and sandals in the cold, and likewise, most people will not wear a large overcoat and gloves when it's 90 degrees outside.

Understanding the principle of *operational temperatures* will cause us to reset our actions and place our expectations accordingly. It lets us know that opportunities and options will come because God will ensure that the timing is right. The idea around timeless living is worth repeating. Timeless living means choosing to spend your time aligned with the natural pace of a spiritually grounded life that prioritizes relationships, people, and a pace that gives you the margin to invest in what you value.

The fourth principle is that God has provided us with *open seasons*. The verse continues with "winter and summer." It represents a continuum of time that confers a lifespan. Winter and summer are representative of the seasons in our lives. As I continue to age numerically (I say it that way because my mental state is ten years younger than my chronological state), I realize that I have to move on from some things that I have done when I was younger. When I was younger, I would play racquetball for three to four hours a day, four to five days a week. My knees have accumulated wear and tear, though, so now—being in a different season physically—I ride my bicycle for ten to twenty miles on a regular basis. *Open seasons* are God's way of helping us to keep things in the proper perspective when it comes to our situations and circumstances. We are prone to take for granted sunrise and sunset, the changing face of the moon and the changing of seasons, but all these functions are evidence that God is on the throne and keeping His promises. Yes, we are currently experiencing a tri-pandemic. We were consumed with an election process that demanded our attention. Yet all creation preaches a constant sermon, day after day and season after season. It assures us that God's loving care is active, right here and right now. We can trust His word, for as 1 Kings 8:56 (NKJV) states, "Blessed be the Lord, who has given rest to His people Israel, according to all that He promised. There has not failed one word of all His good promise, which He promised through His servant Moses."

The fifth principle is that God has made you an *overcomer of time*. The covenant language continues with "And day and night." The previous two principles dealt with temperatures and seasons. But this principle deals with time beyond the clock on the wall. You are an overcomer of time when you understand God's definition of time. There are two words in the Greek language that define time. The first word is Kairos (pronounced kahee-ros). It means a set or proper time. It is sometimes called "due season." The second word is Chronos (pronounced khron-os). It means a space of time without a set interval. How does that connect? (If I were preaching, I would say I'm glad you asked!) Earthly time limits us to one position. That position is chronological. It denotes the length of time (whether short or long). When you start a new job, you have a probationary period that you must complete before you are eligible for company benefits. When you are an *overcomer of time,* you are not held hostage by such guidelines. God is saying to you, at this very moment, that your pain is not a jail sentence. It is not too late for you to move forward, because He, not your situations, determines your seasons. Your life is the making of a miracle (I do not know about you, but I believe in miracles). Miracles are God's extraordinary that are launched in the ordinary. You can experience a miracle in this time because of your relationship with God. In his book *Made for a Miracle: From Your Ordinary to God's Extraordinary*, Mike Slaughter states, "When the call of Jesus becomes personal, God is no longer just a nominal religious tradition or philosophical idea. This life-defining moment marks the GPS course for the rest of your life." It is at that moment that time moves from our hands to the hand of God. I have come to put my trust and hope in God's word. Joshua 10:13 (NKJV) says, "So the sun stood still, and the moon stopped, till the people had revenge upon their enemies. Is this not written in the Book of Jasher? So the sun stood still in the midst of heaven, and did not hasten to go down for about a whole day." The God who controls nature will cause time to pause on your behalf so that you can experience the healing that He has designed for you.

The final principle is the lynchpin to what was discussed previously, and is embedded in the phrase "shall not cease." On one hand, this speaks of a consistent expectation that God is going to do what God has said He will do. Another view is to understand that because you are in relationship with God, you are *outside of negative impact*. I am not saying that you will not have negative things happen in your life. Jesus said it best: "These things I have spoken to you, that in Me you may have peace. In the world you will have tribulation; but be of good cheer, I have overcome the world" (John 16:33, NKJV). This principle speaks to the fact that negative events will not have the same impact upon you because you have chosen to trust the Lord by faith.

Let me share an experience with you. My maternal grandmother transitioned to be with the Lord in 1986. I had prayed for her complete healing. I knew that she was a woman of faith and that she had lived her life to honor God. She was my benchmark for what it meant to "have faith in God." But my grandmother still died. It pained me greatly and I became angry with God. How could He take my grandmother away from us when she was the pillar of our family? I screamed through tears at God that He did not answer my prayer—a prayer uttered in faith! As we prepared to celebrate her life, though, I read the hospital report about her cause of death. We had not known that my grandmother had stage four colorectal cancer, or that it had spread to her major organs. When I prayed for her complete healing, I did not realize that I was praying a necessary prayer.

While my grandmother may have died unexpectedly, we were saved from the potential of watching her suffer a horrible death. It was a painful moment, yes—but a negative moment that was tempered by the grace of God. The principle of being outside of negative impact does not mean that we will not be impacted negatively; it means we will be provided the grace to handle it. Romans 8:28 (NKJV) states, "And we know that all things work together for good to those who love God, to those who are the called according to His purpose." When negative circumstances invade your territory, *you* determine how much real estate it occupies. You and you alone, because only you can determine how things impact your mind, body, and spirit.

There are three reasons, which we can take from the story of Hagar and Ishmael, why it is not too late for you, and why R.A.S.H.E.K.A. can be healed:

1. **Ishmael was the "child of purpose."** While Isaac was the "child of promise," based on God's covenant with Abraham, God still had a designed purpose for Ishmael. I believe that there are things in life that are not in God's perfect will, but that they are in God's permissive will. The law of Moses represents a design of God's will in perfection. Grace through Christ Jesus represents the blending of God's perfect will combined with His permissive will.

2. **Ishmael received provision because of God's covenant with Abraham.** Ishmael could not be left out of the blessings of God. After all, he was a part of Abraham's seed, and God promised Abraham that He would bless His seed.

3. Ishmael's name means "God hears." Your name has meaning to God, and He values who you are because He created you.

It was not too late for Hagar and Ishmael, and it is not too late for you. Psalm 34:17 (NKJV) says, "The righteous cry out, and the Lord hears, and delivers them out of all their troubles." The very fact that you are reading this book is an indicator that you want the best for yourself. Let me assure you that God wants His best for you, which is more transcending and transformational than you can imagine.

The Recapture

It's not too late:

You have opportunity

You have options

You have proper operational temperatures

You have open seasons

You are an overcome of time

You are outside of the impact of negative occurrences

PART III
The Pathway to Healing

Chapter 6

Dealing with the Necessary

"Then He said to them, 'Thus it is written, and thus it was necessary for the Christ to suffer and to rise from the dead on the third day."

—Luke 24:46 (NKJV)

The pathway to healing involves a three-pronged approach. I call this approach "dealing with the necessary." As I have inferred in earlier chapters, many people live in their pain because they will not confront the things in their lives that cause them pain. Often, theologians and church folk want to act like Jesus was exempt from the everyday pains we feel. Hebrews 4:15 says, "For we do not have a High Priest who cannot sympathize with our weaknesses" (NKJV). I don't know about you, but when I think about the fact that one of his boys betrayed him and the rest of the crew abandoned him in a time of need—that is real hurt. During that moment, as Savior, he followed God's command and God Himself left Him in the crucible of pain—the pain of the cross. Jesus demonstrated the power of staying the course. His explanation to the people that caused Him pain is the ammunition we need to walk in the pathway of healing. Why is this important? Think about it—if you walk around as a wounded individual, you will never have complete success or whole relationships. Andrew Carnegie once said, "The position a person occupies in the world depends on the quantity and the quality of the service he renders plus the attitude which he relates to others."

The first aspect of this approach is for you to know the essential. Luke makes a powerful statement when he makes the narrative statement, "Then He said to them, thus it is written." The first point I would like to make is that it is important to understand that the things we contend with in life are fashioned specifically for us individually. In other words, your challenges are tailor-made to propel you to your purpose. Jesus pulls aside a group gripped with fear and tells them that despite the swirling winds around them, a calm will come. There will be a peace tomorrow that is greater than your pain of today. Romans 8:28 is clear, "And we know that all things work together for good to those who love God, to those who are the called according to *His* purpose." It is important to believe that you have what it takes to see your current situation change. That thing that has happened to you (and I am not making light of anyone's circumstance) was put there to propel you to be the best you. It is alright to give yourself permission to come imperfectly before God, because it is God's power that is made perfect in your weakness.

Allow me to share something with you that I have learned: when you deal with the necessary, you know how to tell the difference between what is figurative versus what is actual. Also, there is a big difference between the truth and facts. In my mind, that which is figurative will describe and define the character of a thing. What is actual is based upon your belief system and your core values that guide the intentions of your heart. If you believe that it is better to make war than to make peace, then you will remove figurative and factual results from your actions. If you decided to be a peacemaker, then you will have results that are based on core values that govern your heart. William Barclay paraphrases Matthew 5:9 this way, "Blessed are those peacemakers who produce right relationships in every sphere of life, for they are doing a God-like work." Ask yourself this question: what dictates the choices that you make? When you have a better understanding of the things that are essential to a healthy lifestyle, it will help you to have a better understanding of how it can lead to a place to release the pain of your heart and walk in the place of healing that is according to God's love for you.

We have been surrounded by death during this health pandemic. It has gripped many households across the globe. Amid such adversity, it is important to maintain an uplook that will determine your outlook. When you understand the essential values of a holistic life, your priorities will have a greater meaning. We must be mindful of the fact that healing is achieved through forgiving ourselves and forgiving others. Philip Yancey says "forgiveness alone can stop the cycle of blame, pain as well as vengeance and violence. The meaning of the New Testament word 'forgiveness' is literally to release, to hurl away, to free yourself." Knowing the essential is tied directly to dealing with the necessary and to assume the quest of that insight is a burdensome assignment. The power of God working in humanity is a burdensome work. Acts 15:29 says, "For it seemed good to the Holy

Spirit and to us, to lay upon you no greater burden than these necessary things." The pathway to healing takes work. I shared with my children when they were growing up that "success" only comes before "work" in the dictionary because of its alphabetical sequence. In his book *A Promised Land*, former President Barack Obama states, "my mother had always been quick to remind me that there's a direct link between doing your work and having your wishes come true."

The second approach to dealing with what is necessary for the pathway to healing is what I have deemed "owning the experience." Many of us want to omit the bad experiences in our lives rather than owning them. The Reverend Dr. Cynthia Bourgeault is a member of The Contemplative Society. She states, "Wisdom is not knowing more, but knowing with more of you, knowing deeper." It is imperative that you own all the experiences in your life—the good, the bad, and the indifferent. I do not know about you, but I love all of me. Yes, there are times when I do not like the things I do, but I love all of me. Love does not stick its head in the sand of isolation and detachment but engages by offering wise choices and compassionate counseling. Love looks in the mirror and makes an honest assessment of what it sees. Jesus continues the dialogue in this "circle of hurt" by stating, "and it was necessary for the Christ to suffer." When we own the experience, we gain insight into its purpose. While we may not want to believe it, there is a purpose behind everything that transpires in our lives. We are all either in a challenging season or will be in one soon. Life can either bring it gently, or it can hit like an unexpected tsunami.

Healing for R.A.S.H.E.K.A.

There is a picture in my office at home that I framed years ago. It shows a black bear wearing a scarf, a hat, and gloves (bears don't need to wear winter clothing because they hibernate). The caption reads, "Lord, what would you have me to learn from this experience?" That picture serves as a reminder to me that circumstances should not cause me to cry "why me Lord?!" It is easy to act like a victim when we are in pain. I have also learned that pain is not my enemy. As I am caring for my mother during this time of her life, I am reminded that pain is a sign that something is wrong. Your experience of pain will provide insight and life lessons that lead you to a pathway to healing if you allow it to do so. The longer we live, it becomes more obvious that life is full of repetitive patterns that give us déjà vu moments. Reality (sometimes in the form of pain) is trying to send a signal to our hearts and soul. What we must realize is that our ability to heal cannot depend on anyone's choices but our own, and the process starts with us.

C. S. Lewis says, "Courage is not simply one of the virtues, but the form of every virtue at the testing point." Pain provides a testing point that will help you to produce purpose and keep you focused on the pathway of healing. As Friedrich Nietzsche said, "What does not kill me, strengthens me." I have tried over the years to mask my pain and cover it up in so many ways. I tried with relationships, social connections, recreational activities, and many other avenues. As a believer in Christ, I know that pain is a tool that God will use to "kill my flesh." The Apostle Paul says it this way, "The mind governed by the flesh is death, but the mind governed by the Spirit is life and peace" (Romans

8:7 NIV). We cannot allow pain to govern our minds but allow God's Spirit to show us a way to life and peace. So, owning the experience calls for us to understand the place of pain and purpose, but it also calls for us to allow them both to birth a passion in our lives. What are you passionate about? What burns inside of you each and every day and blazes a fire in your heart? Passion should drive you to want more knowledge and to become better in manifesting the purpose in your life. When we remember and remind ourselves of the truth every day, we will stand strong knowing that when God is for us, nothing can be against us. Samuel Johnson, an eighteenth-century writer said, "People need to be reminded more often than they need to be instructed." Passion provides a level of certainty that bubbles up from within you and can lead you to be reflective as to the source of your pain. Certainty is defined as having confidence, freedom from doubt, and assurance. God wants to birth an anointing in you so you can reposition your corporate setting, your community setting, and your internal settings simultaneously. Ecclesiastes 8:5 says, "He who keeps his command will experience nothing harmful; And a wise man's heart discerns both time and judgement" (NKJV).

The third prong to dealing with the necessary is simply walking in the ending. I know you just said to yourself, that does not make sense. So let me explain. When you deal with the necessary—which places you on the pathway to healing—you are no longer sticking your head in the ground like an ostrich. There are times when you are engaged in a situation, circumstance, or condition and you cannot see the end result. There are times when you put in so many hours at work and you are sitting in your fifth meeting and it is only Tuesday! Jesus concludes the dialogue with his group, who are weary, worn, and wrangling with doubt by saying, "and to rise from the dead on the third day." As a journalism major, I was taught the power of conjunctions in syntax. When Jesus plops an "and" in your life, He is singing the hook from "Ride Out by Rare Essence" and DJ Kool: "hold up, wait a minute!" The "and" in the song's lyrics creates a reversal of what was initially stated. Do you know what happens when you walk in the anointing that God has placed on your life? Weapons of warfare will come against you to try to stop you. Count on the fact that weapons of opposition will come, but they will not prosper. How do I know this? I saw that ending scripture and heard Fred Hammond sing it wonderfully in the song entitled "No Weapon Formed Against Me." He stated, "No weapon formed against me shall prosper/It won't work/God will do what he said he would do/He will stand by his word/And he will come through." Andrew Jackson was quoted as saying, "One man with courage makes a majority." That conjunction in the song's lyrics is powerful because it brings a reversal and then starts a revival in your life. When you are walking in the ending, you are a person with a vision. Without a vision, a person will waste their life. But with a clear vision, they are a force to be reckoned with. When you can see the end of a circumstance while you are still experiencing the pain of it, you are looking beyond the moment of time with a hope that will bring healing.

In Romans 8:15, Apostle Paul states, "I consider that our present sufferings are not worth comparing with the glory that will be revealed in us" (NIV). The revival that will take place in your life will shake you up and wake you up from the "dead things" around you. A reckoning will take place that will create a desire to move the needle on your pain! Do not be afraid to make decisions against yourself or to go against your better judgment. Do not just make a living, make a life! Do not just earn a paycheck; create financial streams that leave a legacy. Go after the passions God has put in your heart, and allow the world to watch God burn through your life! When you combine the reversal with the revival and the reckoning, you get a reconciled individual. Being reconciled is more like singing a song with powerful lyrics that move you to tears. It's less like a mean-looking face and more like a big smile. It is a decision to rest in God and find joy in Him in all circumstances. If you let your circumstances define the way you see God, you are a prisoner of perspective. Even worse, a prisoner of your past mistakes. But, if you let God define the way you see your circumstances, it will create an oxymoron and you become a prisoner of hope. Standing up to stress means staying faithful in your relationships, being disciplined to handling your responsibilities each day, working hard, and maintaining moral and spiritual focus. If you have the right inner circle and a strong personality, you will default to good character and a positive attitude. Dust yourself off. Modify your game plan. Deal with the necessary and do not make the mistake of putting a period where God placed a comma.

The Recapture

Dealing with the Necessary

Knowing the Essential:

Fashioned for You

The Difference Between Figurative and Factual

<u>Owning the Experience:</u>

Purpose

Pain

Passion

<u>Walking in the Ending:</u>

Reversal

Revival

Reckoning

Chapter 7

Helpful Thoughts for Continued Healing

"For I know the thoughts that I think toward you, says the Lord, thoughts of peace and not of evil, to give you a future and a hope."

—Jeremiah 29:11 (NKJV)

Coming to a place of healing is a journey. It takes commitment and it takes work. It is vital that you put some things in place that build your infrastructure. For example, I begin each morning in prayer, reading, meditation, and music. It is important for me to do so because it helps me to stay grounded and positive. How do these areas help me to stay grounded and positive? Prayer allows me to communicate my heart to God. As I communicate my thoughts and God communicates with me, I release negative energy and take in God's energy. I read my Bible and professional subject matter books every day. This increases my knowledge and provides me context that helps me to structure my thoughts accordingly. I meditate on what I have read and my time with God through a listening ear, which helps me when I encounter various situations throughout my day.

As an avid reader, I have learned over time of the importance of comprehension and repetition. They are important because with them, I not only absorb and digest the material, I am also able to develop a practical response as well. This book may have introduced you to concepts that are new to you. While I share my thoughts in this closing chapter on the importance of the healing process, I also want to offer some of my own practical response materials that guide me on my journey of healing. Most people know that communication is the key in relationships. But even the best of us will live our lives in a manner, from time to time, that demonstrates otherwise. Now that you have read this material, allow the material to read you. I often share with people that it is important for you to read your Bible, but it is more important for your Bible to read you. The same concept applies to any reading material that edifies or builds your spirit, mind, and body.

My way of navigating the hard terrain toward healing involves a principle that was invoked in my life about fifteen years ago. I call it the "Resurrection Principle." The scripture says that Jesus was in the grave but rose on the third day. I have a rule of thumb patterned after Jesus' time in the grave to His resurrection from the dead. Depending upon the circumstance, I have three hours, three days, three weeks, or three months to work myself to a place of healing. On the first leg, I am allowed to have a pity party. That is what the first group of disciples did after Jesus' death. They were held up in the house by fear and sadness and were depressed. I am allowed to have a pity part for the first leg of my process. During the second leg, I must begin to execute a plan of action. I believe that a part of God's plan for Jesus while He was in the grave was to preach to the spirits in prison (I Peter 3:19). So, while all seemed lost to the disciples, Jesus was executing the plan of God. On the final leg, it is vital to operate with power that is infused by relationship with God. The text says, Jesus got up with all power. That being the case, I can get up with all power. The Resurrection Principle will propel you to fold up the grave clothes that you were wearing, exit the death chamber that you occupied, and share your revival with all of those who engage you as you walk in the power of your healing.

In my book *Move the Needle: Getting Past the Things That Hinder Your Success*, I shared the following story:

I heard a story once about a frog that was merrily hopping his way through a field. One hop landed him in a giant hole. He found out quickly that he did not have the ability to hop his way out of his predicament. For a while he sat there and planned his demise. He figured that the elements of nature were going to overtake him eventually. But he then decided that if he were going to die, he would die trying. So, he kept trying to get out of the hole, and after focusing on that goal with one hop at a time, he eventually succeeded. When he landed back in the field, he decided to look back in the hole. He was astonished at what he saw: a pile of dirt at the bottom of the hole that he had unknowingly added to after each failed hop, until finally it was high enough for him to get out. One by one, each hop got him to a position of success.

We are experiencing a global health pandemic, a national economic crisis, and the pandemic of racial injustice. We witnessed a presidential debate (debacle is a better description) in which the sitting executive of the United States would not denounce white supremacy, but rather "dog whistled" to hate groups by saying "stand down and stand by." As an African American man, I am pained for my children and grandchildren. I have a grave concern for my sons and grandsons because they are black and male. So, it is important for me to put some "life exercises" in place so that I can remain focused on my purpose in life. Like the frog in the story, if I am going to die—I am going to die trying.

As I contend with racial disparity issues within myself, I have found some practical responses (and there are many) that assist me in my roundedness effort. Please be mindful that the following are suggestions. Because each person's healing journey is based on the individual, I encourage you to develop/find practical responses that fit you (whether it is the aforementioned or the following).

Howard Zehr, the author of *Changing Lenses: Restorative Justice for Our Times*, offers an outline on Ten Ways to Live Restoratively. An additional practical response I would like to share is a quote from W. E. B. DuBois in his book *The Gift of Black Folk: The Negroes in the Making of America*:

> Listen to the Winds, O God the Reader, that wail across the whip-cords stretched taut on broken human hearts; listen to the Bones, the bare bleached bones of slaves, that line the lanes of Seven Seas and beat eternal

tom-toms in the forests of the laboring deep; listen to the Blood, the cold thick blood that spills its filth across the fields and flowers of the Free; listen to the Souls that wing and thrill and weep and scream and sob and sing above it all. What shall these things mean, O God the Reader? You know. You know.

As we have journeyed through these thoughts, there has been an underlying process that is based on the law of seedtime and harvest. God is committed to seeing you healed for a variety of reasons. Every act of life since your birth has operated by the seed principle—springing from good seeds or bad seeds you have sown. Most of us are not consciously aware of the seeds that we plant daily. To overcome life's problems, reach your potential, and see your life become fruitful, multiplied, and replenished (financially, physically, spiritually, or otherwise), sow the seed of God's promise in the soil of your need.

You are no longer a *Run Away Soul Hurt Every Kind Away*—you are now a *Refreshed Anointed Soul Healed Every Kind Away*! Welcome to the refreshed and restored you. I am excited about the impact that you will have on the world from your healthy position.

Sources

Scriptures marked NIV are taken from the New International Version®. Copyright © 1973, 1978, 1984, 2011 by Biblica, Inc.™. All rights reserved.

Scriptures marked NKJV are taken from the New King James Version®. Copyright © 1982 by Thomas Nelson. All rights reserved.

Scriptures marked TLB are taken from The Living Bible copyright © 1971 by Tyndale House Foundation. Used by permission of Tyndale House Publishers Inc., Carol Stream, Illinois 60188.

Unless otherwise indicated, scripture quotations are from the Holy Bible, King James Version. All rights reserved.

About the Author

Joseph K. Williams Sr. is an ordained Baptist minister with over thirty years of ministerial experience. He is a community builder who is an expert at building collaborative relationships between government agencies, corporations, faith communities, and the community at large. He currently serves as the CEO of Bridge of Hope, LLC, which works to help companies understand community thinking, and as a senior program director with Enterprise Community Partners. Previously, he served the senior community as CEO of Emmaus Services for the Aging and as the state president of AARP DC.

Rev. Williams works to empower people and communities through guidance and resources that enrich their core elements. The bestselling author of *Move the Needle*, he is a native of Washington, DC, and currently lives in the District of Columbia. He has three children and six grandchildren.

Learn more at www.bridgeofhopellc.com

CREATING DISTINCTIVE BOOKS WITH INTENTIONAL RESULTS

We're a collaborative group of creative masterminds with a mission to produce high-quality books to position you for monumental success in the marketplace.

Our professional team of writers, editors, designers, and marketing strategists work closely together to ensure that every detail of your book is a clear representation of the message in your writing.

Want to know more?
Write to us at info@publishyourgift.com
or call (888) 949-6228

Discover great books, exclusive offers, and more at
www.PublishYourGift.com

Connect with us on social media

@publishyourgift

www.ingramcontent.com/pod-product-compliance
Lightning Source LLC
Chambersburg PA
CBHW071906070526
44583CB00016B/1867